John

'R,

Twister!

by Bill Haduch

DUTTON CHILDREN'S BOOKS • NEW YORK

For T.W.S., who really knew how to spin

Discovery Communications, Inc.
John S. Hendricks, *Founder, Chairman, and Chief Executive Officer*
Judith A. McHale, *President and Chief Operating Officer*
Michela English, *President, Discovery Enterprises Worldwide*
Marjorie Kaplan, *Senior Vice President, Children's Programming and Products*

Discovery Publishing
Natalie Chapman, *Vice President, Publishing*
Rita Thievon Mullin, *Editorial Director*
Tracy Fortini, *Product Development, Discovery Channel Retail*
Heather Quinlan, *Editorial Coordinator*

Discovery Kids™, which includes Saturday and Sunday morning programming on
Discovery Channel®, Discoverykids.com, and the digital showcase network, is
dedicated to encouraging and empowering kids to explore the world around them.

Discovery Channel® and Discovery Kids™ are trademarks of Discovery
Communications, Inc.

Published in the United States by Dutton Children's Books,
a division of Penguin Putnam Books for Young Readers
345 Hudson Street, New York, NY 10014

Editors: Karen Lotz and Amy Wick • Designer: Leah Kalotay

Printed in USA • First Edition
ISBN: 0-525-46310-0

The Day the Sky Turned Green

At age 11, Brianna was on her own for the very first time. As she arrived at camp and met her cabin mates, she felt excited. Two weeks. A million new things to see and do.

Brianna had been too busy to notice the weather, but now the sky seemed way too dark for 5:30 in the afternoon. As the new friends sat down to dinner, a storm hit hard. The lightning and thunder were constant. Wind poured through the screens. "It's just a storm," the counselor said. "Let's eat." But no one could eat. And it was too loud to talk. The lights flickered. Then they went out.

The shouts of another counselor filled the dining hall. "Everybody up! Follow me!" Brianna found herself running across a lawn. Heavy, horizontal rain splattered her face like a hundred garden hoses. Hard pellets of hail stung her arms and legs. The wind made it hard to run, but soon the group bounced and hustled into the bottom level of the camp's boathouse and slammed the door behind them. Brianna was soaked. She grabbed the counselor's arm and demanded, "WHAT IS GOING ON?"

"It's just a storm," the counselor answered. Suddenly the door blew back open. Brianna could see that the sky outside was a strange green color. "This is NOT just a storm!" she yelled above the roar. Then suddenly it was over. The roar disappeared like an echo. The rain stopped, and the sky turned bright blue. Outside, the camp buildings were still standing. But in the nearby woods, trees were shattered and splintered like toothpicks. "Yes," the counselor admitted, "it was a tornado. We got a warning by radio just before the lights went out. We didn't want anyone to panic."

Brianna felt kind of smart. "I knew it wasn't just a storm," she said.

The Fastest, Most Violent Wind on Earth

Only the biggest twisters have the power to leave paths of destruction like this.

IT'S A TWISTER!

A twister is a tornado—a wildly spinning column or funnel of air that comes from the bottom of a thunderstorm, or from the bottom of a cloud that's almost a thunderstorm. The funnel can swing and hop in all directions, but it's not officially a tornado until it touches the ground.

IT'S FAST!

No one has ever measured the speed of a tornado's whirling winds with traditional weather instruments.

The tornado either wrecks the instruments or misses them. In 1999, a university professor bounced a radar beam off a funnel and measured a 318-mile-per-hour wind—the fastest wind ever recorded.

IT'S POWERFUL!

A tornado can pack a punch more than 16 times stronger than a hurricane. That's why it can twist steel girders and move freight trains. The power is in the wind speed. Scientists still don't know if the funnel itself has a strong suction.

IT'S COMMON, YET RARE!

There are 1,000 tornadoes in the U.S. every year. They have been reported in every state and in every month. But as weather systems, they are small and don't last long. Most people have never seen one.

Flying debris and broken glass are the biggest killers in a tornado.

IT'S DIFFERENT EVERY TIME!

A tornado can be skinny and almost transparent or a mile wide and dark as night. It can last a few seconds or several hours. It can travel a few feet or hundreds of miles.

IT'S WEIRD!

There are many strange stories about tornadoes. But this has to be one of the strangest: In 1996, a drive-in theater was hit by a tornado—while it was showing the movie *Twister*.

5

How the Wind Gets All Wound Up

Mt. Everest is the highest mountain on earth, but a cumulonimbus cloud can easily reach as high as TWO Mt. Everests.

What can a bath and a search for a snack teach you about tornadoes? More than you think!

Take a nice hot bath, and while you're still warm, damp, and barefoot, open your refrigerator door to look for a tempting snack. No, wait! Forget the snack! Notice a cool breeze on your warm feet? Congratulations! You've just demonstrated the basic force behind all weather.

Cool, dry refrigerator air is heavy. It pushes down. The air's heaviness is called "high pressure." Warm, moist bathtub air is lighter. The lightness is called "low pressure." This air rises. The refrigerator air and the air on your feet are trading places, creating wind.

Now think big. The earth has two big refrigerators—the cold polar regions. And it has a big hot bathtub all around the middle—the tropical oceans and wetlands. Plus, there are smaller hot and cold areas all over the globe. Wherever hot and cold meet, the rushing upward and pushing downward begin. You get updrafts and downdrafts. You get weather.

Sometimes an edge of cool, dry air happens to ride up on top of warm, moist air. Guess what the warm air wants to do? RISE, of course. Eventually the hot air blasts a hole through the overhanging cold air and WHOOSH! it rockets skyward in a hot, moist stream. This is an updraft. At the same time, a stream of cold air rushes downward to take its place. This is a downdraft. Together, updrafts and downdrafts create huge clouds called cumulonimbus (kyew-mew-low-NIM-bus). They may billow up to 12 miles top to bottom (remember, think BIG!).

From a distance, a cumulonimbus might look like puffy white cotton balls. Looking up at the cloud from underneath, all you'd see is black. Sunlight can't get through.

It may be 80, 90, or 100 degrees in your backyard, but at the top of a cumulonimbus, it can easily be 112 degrees BELOW zero. This 200-degree difference is why the updrafts and downdrafts are so strong. Separate, high-level horizontal winds up there often blow the top off the cloud and create the classic "anvil" shape.

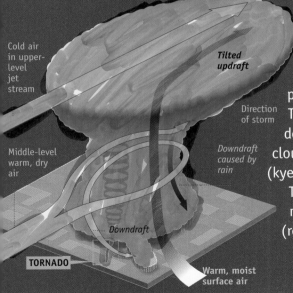

Cold air in upper-level jet stream

Tilted updraft

Direction of storm

Middle-level warm, dry air

Downdraft caused by rain

Downdraft

TORNADO

Warm, moist surface air

While some details of how monster tornadoes develop are still a mystery, much is known about how these twisters form.

Birth of a Twister

A cumulonimbus is also called a "thunderhead." Inside, there's a huge busy area, called a cell, where the warm, moist updraft blasts up through the colder air at about 150 miles per hour. When the updraft cools, it releases moisture, tumbles over, and creates a downdraft. This up/down action often generates the giant electrical sparks we call lightning.

Big Opportunity for Some Future Weather Scientist

Q. Why do about half of mesocyclones form funnel clouds?

A. No one has yet figured that out.

The moisture, falling in the downdraft, pelts the ground as rain or frozen hailstones—or gets snatched up again by the updraft, sometimes taking several updraft/downdraft trips before falling to the ground. Sometimes hailstones can grow larger than baseballs before falling. *Ouch!*

The thunderhead also creates wind. The 150-mph updraft sucks surface air toward the cell. Downdrafts throw air back to the ground, where it scatters away from the cell.

This is a thunderstorm, full of lightning, wind, rain, and maybe hail. There are about 100,000 thunderstorms in the

A funnel cloud is not called a tornado until it touches the ground.

United States every year. Of these, about 2,000 have an added scary feature—the meso-cyclone (meh-zo-SIGH-clone).

What makes a mesocyclone start whirling? Giant wheels of air are always rotating in the atmosphere. Scientists now think that the cells may start to spin when the updraft of an approaching thunderstorm sucks in air from one of these rotating wheels.

A mesocyclone occurs when the whole cell starts to rotate like a giant carousel. Sometimes the whole thunderhead rotates along with it. By itself, a mesocyclone causes no damage. The problem is what sometimes happens next.

Inside about half of mesocyclones, a smaller spinning area develops. This smaller area spins much faster than the big mesocyclone. It begins to look like a funnel as it spins and narrows and lengthens. Sometimes this high-speed spinning funnel stretches long enough to reach the ground. If it does, you have yourself a tornado!

9

When Pigs Fly

Tornado winds are so strong that they can pick things up, give them rides, and put them down. Sometimes objects. Sometimes animals. Sometimes gently. Sometimes with deadly force.

It's the wind that performs the stunts. Speeds can reach over 300 miles per hour, whirling in a tight circle. But "whirling" is too weak a word. It RIPS.

In Kansas, a tornado launched an entire herd of cattle into the air. From a distance, onlookers thought it was a flock of birds.

In 1947, a Texas homeowner went to his front door during a storm. He and the door were lifted up and over the treetops.

NEXT
1 MILE

His friend inside came to the door to see what happened. HE got lifted up over the treetops, too. The two men landed with minor injuries 200 feet away. The wind was still so strong that the men had to crawl in the

Egg sighting! Amid a twister's destruction, a carton of eggs lands safely.

blinding dust back to the house. The house was gone, but the floor was still there, along with a lamp and a couch. On the couch huddled the owner's wife and two kids. They were not hurt.

A May 1986 report from China describes how a group of 12 schoolkids got caught in a tornado's winds, flew 12 miles, and fell into some soft sand. No injuries.

WHAT'S WITH THE SOFT LANDINGS?

The cloud that brings a tornado also brings a mishmash of wild, powerful updrafts, downdrafts, and wind in all directions. These wild winds work with the tornado, work along with each other, work separately, cancel each other out, and do other amazing things that defy gravity, as well as the imagination.

Tornadoes come in all sizes, shapes, and colors. Here's how some eyewitnesses have described what they've seen:

a rope
a pencil
a carrot
an upside-down bell
a black blur
a wide black blur
a wisp
white against a black sky
black against a white sky
a garden hose
a dog chasing its tail
boiling clouds
a witch's boiling cauldron
a snake
an hourglass
an elephant's trunk
a balloon
a candy cane
a giant lawnmower
a spinning top
a barbershop pole

Hot Air: Twister Myths

Twister Tongue Twister

In *The Wizard of Oz*, whic[h] witch wished which wicked wish?

For 2.5 million years of human history, tornadoes were a complete mystery. Every once in a while, a weird, snakelike thing dropped out of the sky, wrecked stuff, and then disappeared. That's about all we knew.

There were no cameras to record what a tornado looks like or does. There was no radar looking inside the clouds. Weather satellites? Not invented yet. Professors getting up close with weather instruments? Forget about it.

In fact, there wasn't even a moving picture of a real tornado until 1951. No one had ever been in the right place at the right time with a movie camera.

Until recently almost everything we knew came from witness reports, stories passed around, and looking at damage. As a result, a lot of wacky information got passed around:

A Straw Shot into a Fence Post is not caused by some magical force. Instead, the wind spreads apart the wood grains, and a straw simply blows in. Then the grains snap shut—instant tourist attraction!

Most Tornadoes Come at Night. Nope. Thanks to afternoon heat, more than half develop between 3 P.M. and 6 P.M. Almost 90 percent come between 1 P.M. and 9 P.M. Check the weather report and say good night.

Heading for the Hills won't work. Stories that tornadoes won't climb mountains or cross rivers (or cut through cemeteries!) are bunk. Tornadoes can go anywhere clouds go. In 1998, for example, a tornado rolled over a river and dashed up the 300-foot cliff that overlooks Pittsburgh.

Twister Tongue Twister

The sun shines on shop signs until cyclones suck the signs off Mrs. Smith's fish-sauce shop.

Vacuum Cleaner Action is probably overrated. Tornado funnels may have some suction, but scientists now say that at ground level it's probably not strong enough to suck the feathers off a chicken or all the water out of a swimming pool. Wild winds cause most tornado stunts.

Fighting Tornadoes with Weapons is a waste of time. Arrows, guns, jet planes, and bombs have all been tried or considered. Hey, everyone needs one last mad act before getting blown into the next county.

Tornadoes Never Come in Winter. Wrong. Tornadoes happen anytime. In the U.S., since 1916 there have been only five tornado-free months: January 1950, October 1952, December 1963, November 1976, and January 1985.

Q: Was Elvis Presley ever in a twister?

A: Yes! When little "El" was 15 months old, in 1936, a huge tornado came through his hometown of Tupelo, Mississippi, and killed 235 people. But not Elvis.

13

Seen One, You Haven't Seen

PICK A COLOR

Tornadoes pick up color from the ground. At first, a funnel cloud is often white with water vapor. If it touches down in an ocean or lake, it may stay white. Freshly plowed fields can make a tornado brown or reddish. Sand turns them yellowish. Dust and debris give twisters a gray/black color.

Sometimes a tornado and the sky around it are strangely green.

Freshly mowed lawns? Nope... Scientists say hailstones can act like prisms and scatter late-day sunlight as a green color.

KINDA SORTA LIKE A TORNADO

Hot air and cold air can curl around each other as they trade places, taking lightweight materials for a spin. Whirling dust creates "dust devils." Farmers' fields make "hay devils." "Ash devils" spin in a volcano's plume. "Fire devils" can be seen in forest fires. "Steam devils" twirl in the morning mist. None are tornadoes, and they don't turn into tornadoes.

Twister
Tongue Twister
A tiny twister tied a tie tighter to tidy her tiny tail.

SKINNY WHIRLING WEAKLINGS

Ships have sailed through them; farm animals have walked through them. Depending on where they whirl, these weaker tornado cousins are called waterspouts or landspouts. They

A dust devil in a dry African lake bed.

Them All

orm early and mysteriously in a thunderstorm, vithout a mesocyclone. They're usually not too trong, but watch out—real tornadoes crossing vater are also called waterspouts.

SOMETIMES YOU DON'T EVEN NEED THE THUNDER

Occasionally tornadoes form in clouds that ren't quite thunderheads. These twisters, some-imes called "gustnadoes," are usually weak and hort-lived.

TORNADOES OF THE SILVER SCREEN

The Wizard of Oz was made in 1939, before any-ne had ever filmed a real tornado. Working vith still pictures and witnesses' descriptions, the moviemakers used a 35-foot tapered tube of muslin fabric swinging from a crane to depict a twister. That big hanging sock remained Hollywood's most life-like tornado for 57 years, until the

Weak waterspout or dangerous tornado? A ship in the Gulf of Mexico seems about to find out.

movie *Twister*. The computer-generated tornado for *Twister* took 10 weeks to design. Two jet engines blew foam chunks across the screen to show debris. And filming through a rain-splattered windshield helped camouflage anything that didn't look real.

15

They Sound Scary, and They Feel Even Worse

More than anything else, people say a tornado sounds like the deep pulsing roar of a freight train. In fact, where tornadoes are common, people get tired of hearing that description. They groan whenever some poor tornado victim says "freight train" in a TV-news report.

Maybe it IS time to add a little variety to our twister lingo. Before the freight train was invented, a Pennsylvania mountain man said a tornado sounded like Niagara Falls. Others have compared it to a hundred jets taking off, a chain saw in a wet log, and the hum of a trillion giant bees.

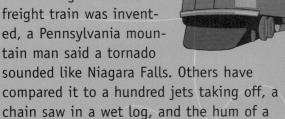

So what makes all this noise? It seems that a twister may be quite a lightning generator. Some reports say lightning flashes constantly

Some reports say a tornado's roar comes from constant thunder in the funnel.

If you're close enough to FEEL a tornado, then you're TOO CLOSE.

within the funnel itself. Constant lightning would mean constant thunder. Hey, that WOULD sound like a freight train. Oops. Sorry.

The only thing worse than hearing a tornado is feeling one. People who have been caught in a twister's path say the updrafts make it hard to breathe. Survivors report feeling that the tornado tried to turn them inside out, that their heads almost exploded, and that their ears wouldn't stop popping. Feeling glued in place is another common complaint. But that's probably just fear. Not much stays glued in place during a tornado.

A TWISTER IN HIS FACE

Will Keller, a Kansas farmer, gained fame in 1928 for looking up into a twister's funnel and surviving. He was on his way into a storm cellar when the funnel passed directly overhead. Here's part of what he told a Kansas weatherman: "It seemed as though I could not breathe. There was a screaming, hissing sound coming directly from the end of the funnel. There was a circular opening about 50 or 100 feet in diameter and extending straight upward for a distance of at least one-half mile. The walls of the opening were rotating clouds, and the whole was made brilliantly visible by constant flashes of lightning which zigzagged from side to side. Had it not been for the lightning, I could not have seen the opening or any distance into it."

17

There's something about long, slithering tubular things that gives humans the creeps—and yet fascinates us. Snakes. Octopus tentacles. Tornadoes. Could it be the weird, sinister ways these things move?

A tornado's got all the weird moves. It cruises along at the speed of the cloud that brings it—usually about 30 miles an hour. But some clouds stand still; others race along at 70.

The funnel has a mind of its own. It swings and sways, sometimes in circles, sometimes zigzagging. It can disappear and reappear, or bounce up and down.

A funnel is usually on the ground for about 10 minutes. But sometimes they touch down just for a second. In 1925, one may have lasted for $3\frac{1}{2}$ hours.

The National Weather Service estimates the strength and wind speed of a tornado by examining the damage it did. Then it ranks the tornado on a scale of F0 to F5.

An incredible tornado causes incredible devastation: the aftermath of an F5 tornado in Oklahoma in May 1999.

THE FUJITSU SCALE

If a tornado causes damage like this:	This is what scientists call it:	And the wind in the funnel was about:
Chimneys, tree branches, and signboards damaged. Shallow-rooted trees pushed over.	F0—Gale Tornado	40–72 mph
Roof shingles blown off. Mobile homes pushed off foundations or overturned. Moving cars pushed off road. Attached garages possibly destroyed.	F1—Moderate Tornado	73–112 mph
Entire roofs torn from houses. Mobile homes demolished. Boxcars pushed over. Large trees broken or uprooted. Light objects fly through air.	F2—Significant Tornado	113–157 mph
Walls torn from solidly built houses. Trains overturned. Forests uprooted. Heavy cars lifted and thrown.	F3—Severe Tornado	158–206 mph
Solidly built houses leveled. Some structures blown for a distance. Cars and large objects fly through the air.	F4—Devastating Tornado	207–260 mph
Strong wooden houses lifted up, carried, and wrecked. Car-sized objects fly 100 yards or more. Bark pulled off trees. Steel-reinforced concrete structures badly damaged.	F5—Incredible Tornado	261–318 mph

Only in movies would a meteorologist say, "An F5 tornado is headed this way!" No one knows the ranking until the twister is over.

Only 1 percent of tornadoes are classified F4 or F5. About 24 percent are F2 or F3. Most tornadoes by far—75 percent—are F0 or F1. But even an F1 has faster winds than most hurricanes!

F5 may be the highest ranking scientists ever expect, but there is a ranking of F6. Wind speed would be 319 to 379 mph. They call this the "Inconceivable Tornado."

ESTIMATING TORNADO INTENSITIES

These "F-scale" rankings for tornadoes were developed in 1971 by University of Chicago meteorologist Tetsuya "Ted" Fujitsu. Rankings are assigned by inspecting the damage created by a tornado. Because they're not based on instrument readings, all wind speeds are estimates.

The Tornado Police

Radar helps police pick speeding cars out of traffic. Why shouldn't it help scientists pick speeding tornadoes out of a thunderhead?

It does. While older weather radars were only able to scan clouds for water droplets, newer Doppler radar can also show the water droplets' speed and direction. It can tell scientists whether there's rotation—a mesocyclone—in the cloud. If there is, the scientists start spreading the word: a tornado has a good chance of getting started!

Spreading the word has been a lifesaver. Since the 1970s, the number of tornadoes has stayed about the same, but the number of deaths from tornadoes has dropped sharply. Earlier in the 20th century, it was common for 200 to 1,000 Americans to be killed by tornadoes every year. For the past 20 years, the average has been 69.

Doppler radar is able to detect mesocyclones from a distance of 150 miles. In 1991, the people of Andover, Kansas,

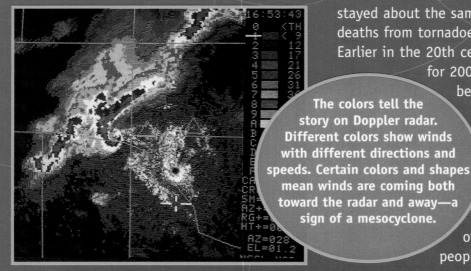

The colors tell the story on Doppler radar. Different colors show winds with different directions and speeds. Certain colors and shapes mean winds are coming both toward the radar and away—a sign of a mesocyclone.

Doppler radar may be housed in a building, in a vehicle, or in a portable unit.

In 1972, the average warning time for tornadoes was less than one minute. Today, Doppler radar can provide as much as 45 minutes of warning. Property may still get banged up, but people have more time to take cover.

had a 45-minute warning about a possible approaching tornado. When the F4 monster finally arrived, it leveled 350 houses. The death toll was 13, all in cars or mobile homes.

Like all radar, Doppler can see in all kinds of weather and even in the dark. Since 1997, the U.S. has had a network of 160 Doppler radar sites all across the country. The continental U.S. and Hawaii are completely covered, along with most of Alaska.

Where the Wind Comes Sweepin' Down the Plain

The bad news? Texas, Oklahoma, Kansas, Nebraska, South Dakota, Missouri, and Iowa have more tornadoes than anywhere on earth. The good news? They also have more tornado experience, experts, and warning systems than anywhere on earth.

The region is nicknamed Tornado Alley, and every April, May, and June, about 20 to 40 tornadoes A WEEK touch down here. It's a great place to study, photograph, and learn how to protect yourself from tornadoes.

What causes this weather with a twist? Geography! To the west are the Rocky Mountains. The air there in spring stays cold as it drifts,

Human spirit survives in Tornado Alley, even when the odds don't work out. After three hits on his house, one resident told the Discovery Channel, "This is our home. We're not going to move. If it blows us away again, we'll build again."

SOUTH DAKOTA

IOWA

NEBRASKA

KANSAS

MISSOURI

OKLAHOMA

TEXAS

TORNADO ALLEY

In the middle of the action is Norman, Oklahoma, the tornado-knowledge capital of the world. It is the site of the National Severe Storms Laboratory, the Storm Prediction Center, the University of Oklahoma's School of Meteorology, the U.S. Doppler Radar Support Center, and many other weather organizations.

high and dry, from the polar regions. To the south, there's the Gulf of Mexico. Air from here is warm, moist, and low. Add the energy of the sun as the spring days grow warmer, and you have a great recipe for tornado soup.

The odds of a particular building getting struck by a twister in Tornado Alley have been calculated at once every 250 years. But people here take no chances. Many dig backyard storm shelters or strengthen areas of their basements. Schools have tornado drills—students rush to basement shelters or interior hallways, where they cover their heads with their hands. And people quickly learn the sound of the town tornado siren.

On the flat plains of Tornado Alley, twisters can often be seen for miles.

Twisting Around the World

The flat, treeless plains of Tornado Alley may be home to the world's most dented Twister Trophy, but twisting has been going on worldwide since time began.

Tornadoes have touched down in all 50 states (though Alaska, Hawaii, and Rhode Island may see only one every decade or so). Japan, Australia, South Africa, Sweden, Switzerland, and Germany also see them. England is said to report more tornadoes for its size than any nation in the world.

Outside the U.S., the most damaging tornadoes take place in Bangladesh and Argentina, where mountains, plains, and warm water create their own mini tornado alleys.

The "world series" of twisters was in April 1974. They called it the "Super Outbreak." In 18 hours, 148 tornadoes touched down in 13 states and provinces from Ontario to Alabama—none of them in Tornado Alley—and 315 people were killed. Tractor-trailers landed on bowling alleys. Small towns were completely flat-

Wisconsin may be more famous for cheese than for tornadoes, but the Badger State still averages about 19 tornadoes a year.

WEST BROOK

tened. Letters and papers from Xenia, Ohio, were found 200 miles away.

The largest, longest-lasting, deadliest twister in U.S. history is thought to be the "Tri-State" Tornado of 1925. It started well east of Tornado Alley and traveled 219 miles through Missouri, Illinois, and Indiana in 3½ hours. It killed 689 people. Witnesses said it didn't look like a funnel at all—just a huge boiling black cloud moving along the ground. Scientists today figure there must have been more than one twister in that cloud.

There will always be property damage, but improved warnings help keep deaths and injuries down in the U.S. It's different elsewhere. In Bangladesh, a single tornado recently killed 1,300 and injured 12,000.

EVER BEEN CAUGHT IN A "WILLY-WILLY"?

You might if you went to Australia. Here's how to say "tornado" in some other languages:

German: Wirbelsturm

Swedish: virvelstorm

Dutch: wervelsturm

Danish: hvirvelstorm

Italian: tornado

Spanish: tornado

French: tornade

Japanese: tatsumaki

Latin: turbo

Gaelic: ioma-ghaoth

Finnish: pyorremyrsky

Turkish: kasirga

Polish: traba powietrzna

Serbo-Croatian: olujni vetar

Hawaiian: makani ka'a wiliwili

Always Looking for Trouble

There aren't more tornadoes these days—there's just more and better tornado reporting.

Thanks to improved equipment and new understanding, today's tornado experts know just where to look and what to look for. The national Doppler radar network can pinpoint cloud rotation, even in the dark.

Armed with computers, weather equipment, portable radar, and cameras, hundreds of storm chasers cruise the plains of Tornado Alley every spring. Most are university professors, students, or government scientists who study tornadoes and report what they find out. TV weather people, journalists, and photographers also hit the roads. But even with the best equipment, storm chasers need luck to see a tornado. Most spend weeks and travel thousands of miles yet never do cross paths with a twister.

A storm chaser's dream. But, is it too close for comfort?

WAIT...IS THAT A TORNADO?

Here's how storm chaser Wayne Curtis summed up a typical Tornado Alley experience for Discovery Channel Online (www.discovery.com):

Total time of tour: more than 5 weeks

Waiting for storm conditions: about 4 weeks

Actually chasing and checking out storms: 9 days

Seeing supercells: 7 days

Seeing two tornadoes: less than 2 minutes

During the tour, Wayne traveled about 4,700 miles. That's like driving across the U.S. one and a half times. That's why storm chasers often complain about the cost of fuel.

CHASING DANGER

The biggest danger in storm chasing is all the driving. The second biggest is standing in an open field and getting struck by lightning.

INTELLIGENCE RULES

When a tornado does appear, chasers use a lot of knowledge to stay safe. Examples: Getting closer than one mile to a tornado is considered crazy. Chasers need to be experts in estimating distance, which is difficult in dust and clouds and wind. Twisters sometimes create illusions that they're standing still when they're actually moving forward. Also, tornadoes sometimes hide behind a wall of rain and hail. This is called "the bear in the cage." Very dangerous.

Portable equipment has greatly improved storm chasers' chances of seeing a twister—but it's still hard to be in the right place at the right time.

Mister Twister

For one kid growing up in New England in the 1950s, weather was a real WOW! The damage and drama of a big tornado became one of Howie Bluestein's earliest memories.

A year later, a hurricane hit Howie's neighborhood. There was damage, flooding, power outages, and more commotion.

Shortly afterward, Howie was just lying around, watching TV. Not too exciting, right? BOOM! A bolt of lightning hit the rooftop antenna, and the TV exploded!

No doubt about it. Young Howie was hooked on the excitement of weather.

Today, Howie is Dr. Howard B. Bluestein, professor of meteorology at Oklahoma University. Besides teaching, he hurries around Tornado Alley filming, measuring, and studying tornadoes. Once he saw nine twisters in one day. He's an expert in portable Doppler radar. He writes books about tornadoes. And when Hollywood was making the movie *Twister,*

Howie was the man they came to see. In fact, the movie's "Dorothy" contraption was based on a real-life version Howie used, called "TOTO."

Howie thinks his early experience with big storms and exploding TVs probably led to the exciting work he does

Scientists like Howie Bluestein add much to our knowledge about tornadoes—knowledge that can help us build safer buildings and protect ourselves.

today. "I'm sure it must have," he says. As a kid, he loved Boston's creative TV weatherman Don Kent, "who explained everything about the weather." Then, beginning at age 11, he had fun learning about electronics, geography, and worldwide weather with a hobby in ham radio. Howie went on to college at MIT, where he got a solid scientific background in electrical engineering. "It was a heavy combination of physics and math," he said. "I didn't shift into meteorology until graduate school." Everything clicked when Howie visited Oklahoma and its extensive weather facilities. He knew he'd found the right place to live and work. For Howie Bluestein, Tornado Alley is home sweet home.

Saving Your Skin

Human control of tornadoes is not going to happen anytime soon. Only in the past few years have scientists even begun to understand what really goes on in a tornado. But our growing knowledge is already helping people live through these most violent of all storms.

Doppler radar and new research have changed forecasting entirely. Seeing cloud rotation from 150 miles away and being able to send earlier warnings will save thousands of lives in the future. And studying what tornadoes actually do to buildings will help make both people and property safer.

Here's some of what we've learned in recent years:

FORGET THE WINDOWS

Even experts used to think tornadoes made buildings explode. They suggested opening windows to equalize the pressure. Now they know going near windows is a terrible idea when a tornado is coming. Flying debris is the biggest killer, and even little pieces of glass can hit you like speeding bullets.

BUILDING A BETTER BUILDING

Here's how a building goes down in a tornado.

First, the wall closest to the tornado falls inward, letting in a huge amount of wind. Second, the roof lifts off. Third, other outside walls fall outward. Architects now believe it's important to have steel fasteners where the walls meet, where the roof attaches, and where the walls meet the foundation. Architects also say:

* Keep windows to a minimum, or at least have storm windows installed.

* Have doors designed to open outward or have extra locks installed. This can help keep them from blowing inward.

ANTIMISSILE DEFENSE

The main idea behind storm safety is protection from flying debris, officially called missiles. Do whatever you can to stay out of their way. An interior hallway or bathroom without windows is a good place to go. An interior hallway in a basement is even better. Better still would be a basement storm shelter with steel-reinforced walls and its own separate roof. Best place of all? An underground storm cellar—missiles pass

right over you. By the way, the old idea about crouching in a building's southwest corner is wrong—it's too close to an outside wall.

Flying debris causes most tornado deaths and injuries. Stay away from windows!

MADE TO MOVE

When it comes to tornadoes, mobile homes have a built-in problem. Because they're mobile, materials and fastening systems are lightweight. Sadly, 50 percent of all U.S. tornado deaths occur in mobile homes. But tornadoes can't and don't seek out mobile homes. It's just that other types of homes are constructed in various ways, so they experience various types of damage. In a mobile-home park, the trailers share the same type of lightweight construction. The damage here doesn't vary—it's often total. If it's meant to be moved, a tornado can move it. That's why it's also a bad idea to stay in a car or bus during a tornado.

Twister
Tongue Twister

In a tornado, the bleak breeze blights the bright blue blossom.

31

Living to Tell About It

Living through a tornado gives you something to talk about. You can annoy people by saying, "It sounded just like a freight train!" You can sell T-shirts that say, "I Survived the Big Blow of (fill in year)." The possibilities are endless. But first you have to stay alive. Uninjured is nice, too. Knowing a few rules can help you protect yourself:

* If a tornado is coming, you MUST seek shelter. An underground shelter is best, and a basement is good. If there's no basement, find an inside bathroom, room, hallway, or closet on the lowest floor, AWAY FROM WINDOWS. Try to keep your head covered.

* If you are at school during a tornado, listen and do what the adults say. Most schools have weather-emergency plans. School gyms, auditoriums, and other open areas tend to have weak roofs and are dangerous. You'll probably be directed to a basement area or an inside hallway. Do whatever you ca to keep your head covered.

* If you are outside and cannot get inside, lie flat in a ditch or ravine. Lie face down and cover your head with your hands. The idea is stay out of the path of flying debris.

* If you are in a car, bus, or mobile home, get o and run to the nearest storm shelter or solid building. If there are no buildings nearby, lie flat in a ditch or ravine as above. Drivers shoul never attempt to outrun a nearby tornado.